Diana Loubaki

Introduction to economic modeling

To André Loubaki and Jeanne Miantéla

Same Author publications

Essai sur l'Economie du développement, Paris, LEN, 2012.
Initiation à la Modélisation Economique, Paris, LEN, 2012.

Presentation

The aim of this book is the development of a universal economic theory. We mean, a theory based on economic problems relate to growth and development. We highlight appropriate analytical tools able to unify economic study of both poor and rich countries. The analysis shows *first*, it can be established a link between growth and development economics through a well being collective criteria which guarantee a positive evolution of the economic systems over time. Therefore, it becomes possible to control economic paths towards their long run locus. *Second*, the analysis begins on poverty and under development dilemmas in order to highlight the mechanics which link growth and development. The purpose of the analysis is the rise of standard economic development theory [Hirschman (1958), Rostow (1960), Lewis (1954)] which fall in the mid 1970s [Krugman (1994)] through its introduction in the growth literature which began with Smith (1776).

.

Introduction

According to WTO[1], in this 21th century, Africa remains the poorest continent in the world because of both its low technological level and its high national debt. Despite of the size of its population which represents 12.5% of the whole world, its production only reaches 3.7% of global GDP. Its contribution to the world trade is only for 1.7% of the whole exchanges. The World Bank's November 15 announces stipulates that, world food crisis began in 2008 keeps accurate until now. Therefore, whereas *per-capita* income in Africa was only nine times lower than that of the OEDC countries in the 1970s, it turns out to be eighteen times lower at the end of the 1990s and this gap keeps increasing over time. Moreover, United Nations' commission report for Africa, stipulates that, 52% of people live with less

---

[1] World Trade Organization

than 1 dollar per day and extreme poverty reaches 43% of urban population against 59% of rural population. In level terms, according to the UNPD, poverty was for about 217 millions of people in 1987 and rises to 291 millions of people in 1998. According to WHO[2], Poverty leads to 300,000 deceases per day in developing countries. Finally, under development and poverty are linked. Therefore, the purpose of this first part of the analysis, is to determinate their causality link. Meaning is it poverty which causes under development? Or is it under development which causes poverty?

Standard economic development theory began in the 1940s. The purpose of the theory was to study growth of the low income countries. It postulated concepts able to allow poor countries stimulate growth as it is the case for developed countries. Among the most famous development economists, we find Roseinstein-Rodan (1943) with the «*big-push*», Lewis (1954) with «*the economic dualism*»,

---

[2] World Health Organization

Hirschman (1958) with «*the balanced growth*» and Rostow (1960) with «*the stages of economic development*». Between the 1940s and the 1950s, standard economic development theory was deeply influential among both economists and policy makers. Yet in the late 1950s, standard development theory rapidly unraveled to the point where in the mid 1970s, it became incomprehensible. Since the mid 1970s, economists have broken through this barrier in a number of fields: international trade, economic growth and finally, development. In the 1950s, although the technical level of the leading development economists was actually quite high enough to have allowed them to do the same thing, the bag of tricks wasn't there. So development theorists were placed in an awkward bind with basically sensible ideas they couldn't quite express in fully worked-out models. And the drift of the economics profession made the situation worse. In the 1940s and even in the 1950s, it was possible for an economist to publish a paper that made persuasive points verbally, without trying up all the loose ends. After 1960s, however, an attempt to publish a paper like Roseinstein-

Rodan's would have immediately gotten a grilling [Krugman (1994)]. In parallel, a rigor is highlighted in growth theory whereas development economics is facing a methodological crisis. Standard development economics is off-set by growth theory which beginnings are back to Smith (1776). The author assumes increasing returns from task specialization. Then over time, Ricardo's comparative advantages theory is related to mathematics models with simulation like Mundel and Flemings. In the beginning of the 20th century, mathematicians like Marshall and Koopmans introduce mathematics and econometrics models in economic analysis. Standard development economics entirely fall because of the lack of mathematicians able to model the analysis proposed. Because development economics was unable to express itself through a well specified model, it lost its credibility. Therefore, the existing frontier between growth and development theories broke. Indeed, after the mid 1970s, required tools for development studies are free. Development can be studied with growth theory tools.

Krugman(1994) relates the history of the development theory with a fresh eyes in order to bring a more explicit explanation. His analysis is a survey in order to renew standard development theory. On the basis of development economics theorists' ideas such as Hirschman (1958) and Roseinstein-Rodan (1943), he establishes high development theory. Keywords' explanation useful to understand both the analytical field used and the development theory are necessary to understand the problem. Under development which is the main worry of the development theory is defined differently depending to the authors. According to Krugman (1994), under development is due to the fact that, some countries have failed to get in a virtuous cycle driven by external economies as it is going. Therefore, they remain stuck in a low level trap. Krugman's discussion is highlighted by imaging a country in which 20,000 unemployed workers are taken from the land and put into a large new shoe factory. They receive wages substantially higher than their previous income in "natura" because investment returns create positive externalities among industries. Consequently, if investment is relates to the other industries, then increasing returns appears. Indeed, increasing returns and circular causation are legitimated by Myrdal (1957). Hirschman (1958) disagree a policy of promoting a few key sectors with strong linkages. Then, moving on to other sectors to correct the disequilibrium generated by these investments, he prefers the "balanced growth" and found a great advocate in Nukse (1953). The relationship between market size and scale returns economies to some firms and not to some others is clearer. Indeed, economies of scale are crucial to Krugman and present to growth theorist such as Allyn Young (1928).

Can we believe to the prevalence of the theory of standard development if the main concepts used have already been found by classics and neoclassical growth economists?. Is it possible to renew a theory which deals without well specified analytical tools?

Those questions are crucial specifically because of the event of the independence of African countries under the great European political power among like France, Great Britain, Belgium and Portugal.

In 1958 at Cambridge University, Rostow asked two questions related to developing countries' growth hypothesis. Those questions are:

Do new independent countries able to stimulate growth and development like the industrial countries?

Do Communism able to help those countries reach the long run growth?

The beginning of the years 90 pointed out, the victory of market based economies on planned based economies and the fall of the economic thought based on Marx communism concept. Therefore, Rostow (1960) is finally based on Smith (1776) economic growth thought. Thus, was it worth speaking partly about growth and development theories? Do growth and development thoughts converge?

Krugman (1994) stipulates that, finally standard development theorists thought does make a lot of sense. Krugman (1994) *high development theory* is a meditation on economic methodology inspired by the history of development economics in which Albert Hirschman appears as a major character. The distinctive features of high development theory come from its explanation of the nature of the positive feedbacks that can lead to self-reinforcing growth or stagnation. Self-reinforcement comes from an interaction between economies of scale at the level of the individual producer and the size of the market. Crucial to this interaction, is some form of economic dualism in which "traditional" production pay lower wages and/or participate in the market less than the modern sector [Lewis (1954)]. The idea is that: modern methods of production are potentially more productive than traditional ones. But their productivity edge is large enough to compensate the necessity of paying higher wages only if the market is large enough. But market size depends on the extent to which modern techniques are adopted. Because, workers in the modern sector earn higher wages and/or participate in the market economy more than traditional workers. Thus, if modernization can be gotten started on a sufficiently large scale, it will be self-sustaining. Otherwise, it will not and got caught in a trap in which the process never gets going. According to growth theorists, the analysis of developing countries low economics levels can be done with endogenous growth tools. Which makes sense, thus the previous existing dualism among the both theories is over. At the results' level, endogenous growth models such as Romer (1986), Lucas (1988), King-Rebelo (1987) and Azariadis-Drazen (1990) can be applied to developing countries.

Exogenous growth theory is unable to explain the existence of developing countries. Because the theory is based on the Solow (1956) growth model where there is convergence among economies in the long run. This property is due to decreasing marginal returns of physical capital. Thus, poor countries grow faster than rich countries and catch them. There aren't theoretical foundations able to explain observed differences among countries in development economics terms because they turn out to be the same in the long run.

In contrast, endogenous growth theory highlights economic differences among countries in development terms. It assumes constants returns in physical capital which creates conditional convergence and no more absolute convergence like before. Under development trap is similar to poverty [Azariadis-Drazen (1990)]. There is confusion between poverty and under development which are finally badly explained. Development theorists associate poor countries economies to under development phenomenon. Whereas, growth theorists associate poor countries economies to the caught in poverty trap. Moreover, economic backwardness or poverty is caused by low incentives to invest in human capital and in R&D[3].

Growth literature studies migration among rural and urban area in the same country on the basis of Lewis (1954), Haque and Kim (1995), Harris-Todaro (1970) and Miyagiwa

---

[3] Research-Development

(1991). Exogenous theory of economic growth is unable to introduce international migrations of the labor force in the analysis. This is due to the equality among countries in economic development term which lets no room to incentives to migrate because the wage rate income of a given country is the same to the other country in the long run [Solow (1956)].

Equivalently, endogenous growth theory is unable to include international migrations in the analysis too. The one sector endogenous growth models like Romer (1986) and Lucas (1988) leave no room for migrations issues.

The brain-drain theory is the one which allows for migrations of the labor forces [Doquier-Marfouk (2006), Docquier-Rapoport (2010)]. International labor mobility in the brain drain models is limited to high skilled labor from developing countries to developed countries only.

The fundamental link between the growth and the brain-drain literatures is established by the assumption that human capital and knowledge accumulations are development economics engines. Therefore, high skilled labor absence in developing countries is due to high incentives to migrate to more developed countries. Coupled to uncertainty in future return of high skilled labor, the poor economy is kept in a poverty trap.

The plan of the book is as follow

Part I : The foundations of the analysis of economic development

   -Chapter 1: Under development and Poverty

   -Chapitre 2: Development and growth

Part II : Growth foundations for development economics

   -Chapter 3: the theoretical foundations of growth and development

-Chapter 4 : Conclusion

The foundations of the analysis of economic development

Under Development and Poverty

1   INTRODUCTION

Since the 1960s, the economic history of Africa is similar to successive tragedies which consequences are disastrous both in economics and in human fields. Before the independence of the African countries, the World Bank chief economist had estimated growth capabilities in Sub-Saharan at higher level than that of Latin America and South Eastern Asia i.e an average growth rate of 7% per year for Sub-Saharan Africa. But, those estimations didn't realize during the period 1965-1995. Whereas, Eastern Asia and pacific growth rates reached more than 5% per year and more than 2% in Latin America, most of the African countries realized negative growth rates only.

Development economics theory main purpose is poor countries growth absence and differ to growth theorists in postulating that development is wider than growth which accounts GDP mostly [Assidon (2002), p.5] whereas development is a vector of qualitative variables to deal with, growth is mostly a quantitative variable measured by the GDP.

This study focuses on Sub-Saharan Africa. Colonization began in 1870s and ended in 1960s. The main European political powers to whom belonged the Sub-Saharan Africa's countries are: France, Great Britain, Portugal, Belgium and Germany which lost its territories after the 2d world war. Colonial system was composed of an administration, a political system, a land lord and a market capital. Colonial territories were the receptors of the manufactured goods brought by the metropolis. There existed an indigenous sector i.e a traditional sector and a modern sector or Occidental. The aim of the first sector consisted on the self sufficiency needs. Whereas the aim of the second consisted on raw materials import and final goods export. The exchange logic was unbalanced because the goods traded were taken back [S. Bruel][4].

The economic development process elaborated in this book mainly focuses on Sub-Saharan Africa's countries because Latin America's countries growth path is in transition between the *take-off* locus and growth locus whereas Eastern Asia countries are in transition between *development* path and *growth*. Therefore Africa's development economic target is a dynamic process over time [Rostow (1960)].

To develop theoretical foundations of growth in poor countries, we refer to the development economics theory and the empirically observed poverty. This analysis

---

[4] Le sud dans la nouvelle économie Mondiale

focuses on the under development debate began in 1950s. This first chapter deals with relationships between under development of productive capacities and poverty. We attempt to determinate the real causality sense i.e we want to know in how far under development of productive capacities causes poverty and in how far poverty causes under development of productive capacities. The proof is provided on the basis of the literature of small firms and growth in order to understand the problem presented above. The analysis also uses endogenous growth methodology. Therefore, there are non efficient firms and poor households in the economic system. When crucial variables are provided by the optimizing behaviors of private investors, then growth is endogenous. Otherwise, it is not. This book presents a series of endogenous growth models.

2 THE LITERATURE OF SMALL FIRMS AND GROWTH

The main difference between micro and small firms in this analysis is based on total employees. When total employees is less than 4 workers, then it is a micro firm denoted MF. Otherwise, when total employees is between 5 and 50, then it is a small firm denoted SF. The aim of this first presentation is to highlight the relationships between poverty and under development on the basis of the economic literature.

Poverty is local when it touches economic agents, this is a micro level. Poverty is global when it is viewed in a larger sense at the scale of the whole country, it is a macroeconomic level. Poverty means to lack of the essential necessary things to live. Poverty is relative among the economic agents of the same country whereas it is absolute when its level is compared to that of the other countries.

An MF/SF firm is a winner if the entrepreneur and the employees have great creative capabilities. They are mostly men [Nichte-Golmark (2009)]. Their environment provides great capabilities of growth generation if the creativity and the diligence of the entrepreneurs are great [Collins-Porras (1994)]. LiedHolm (2002) and Mead-Liedhomn (1998) find that in Africa as well as in Latin America, less than 3% of the MF firms develop to reach more than 4 workers. SF firms have higher probability to contract than to expand. Growth generated is third times higher than employment created [Fajnzylber-Maloney-Rojas (2006)]. If some firms extend and some others doesn't extend, it is due to four characteristics differentials which prevail among the firms. Those characteristics are: the level of education of the entrepreneur which makes him able to learn new technologies of the production process i.e new design and specific knowledge [Burki-Terell (1998), Tan-Batra (1995)]. The second characteristic is professional experience. Parker (1995) proves that the most growing firms in Kenya have less than 7 years of experience. Men have easier access to more career opportunities than women [Rubio (1999)]. In Africa as well as in Latin America, 61% of MF/SF firms are directed by women against 46%-84% in Malawi, in Dominic Republic and in Swaziland [Mied-Liedholm (1998)].

Development economics literature defines a symmetric between men and women in growth draining task. Because both women mobility and rights are lower than that of the men. It is the same thing in the concern of the respective men and women duties in the society. Thus there is a disproportion between men and women in the household [Downing-Daniels (1998)]. Most of the time, woman has a lower education level than men and his fecundity rate is quite high. Children care by the other is not possible because of its opportunity cost compare to the income generated by the household. In the same order of ideas, under development caused by non efficient firms is due to firms' characteristics, to country's development level as well as to firms' age [Mead-Liedholm (1998), Parker (1995), Burki-Terell (1998)]. The other influent factors are administrative formalities due to institutions imperfections in developing countries. This last characteristic is evaluated to up to 55% in Latin America against 45-85% in Easter Asia and 80% in Africa. In conclusion to all the above results, developing countries' firms cause global poverty but not local poverty. Now *we analyze in how far the firms cause local poverty in developing countries.*

Firms cause local poverty when they employ low skilled labor and most of the time it is the case in developing countries [Nichter-Goldmark (2009)]. Daniels (1999),

IDB (1998) and Small (2002) prove that, firms contribution is higher in growth terms than in employees terms. Employment rates are at about 38%, 13% and 11% of total active population respectively in Dominic republic, in Kenya and in Pakistan. For the growth rate, the authors find 40% for Kenya. Therefore, firms contribute more to growth than to employment. The observed low labor productivities result from low incentives to invest in human capital accumulation.

Finally, under development of productive capacities doesn't directly cause local poverty but indirectly. Local poverty is directly caused by low incentives to invest in human capital accumulation. This last quality is the one which explains the most low labor productivities non efficiency added to low income growth rates. Inequalities on capital market access explain low incentives to invest in education. In contrast, under development of productive capacities are mainly due to global poverty. Institutions imperfections decrease firms' necessary power to generate growth and thus create global poverty (see the figure below)

Three key concepts determinate under development of firms' productive capacities and they are:

-Education for all and learning by doing effects, increase labor productivity due both to low education levels and to unskilled professional experience. Human capital increases through externalities in good production and leads to equilibrium in the skills terms.

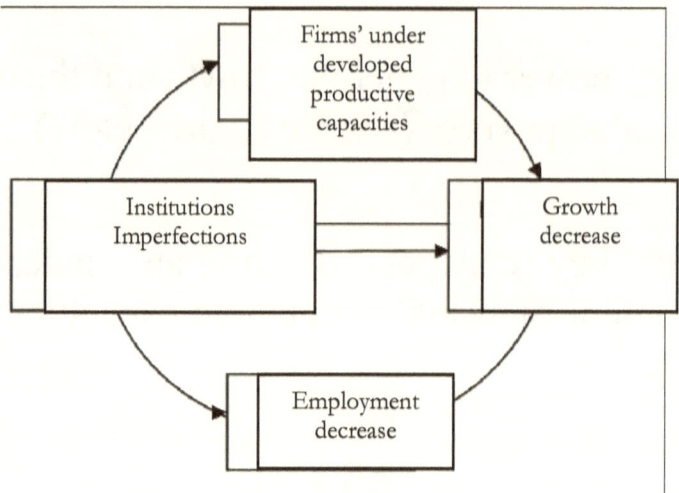

-Women education erases inequalities among sex in growth increase activity through demographic transition which leads to children opportunity increase and then, increase children quality rather than quantity in its choice [Galor-Weil (2000)]

-Democracy and/or subsidies to the firms make the entrepreneurs believe more in their project because of the transparency of the law.

To examine analytically all those parameters in order to study economic development, we use the basic model of Wigniolle et al (2005). The basic model deals with imperfect competition in order to increase human capital in developing countries on the basis of Lewis (1954) and Ranis-Fei (1954). In contrast, this model deals with perfect competition in an endogenous growth and development model.

3   THE ANALYSIS

This part of the analysis model the idea of Krugman (1994) i.e *if 20,000 unemployed workers are taken from the land and put into a large shoe factory, they receive wages substantially higher than their previous income in "natura".*

Indeed, we expose the model

Consider a dual closed economy i.e an economy endowed with two production sectors where the one is traditional, which we assimilate to a MF firm and the other is modern which we assimilate to a SF firm. MF or equivalently, each peasant cultivate his land l eats a part and sell the rest to live. The stock of peasant L is the labor force stock of the economy which works with a quantity of land stock, T. Peasants live only one period. But entrepreneurs of the firms SF live during two periods. Population growth rate moves at a rate n i.e $N_{t+1}=(1+n)N_t$ where $N_t=H_t+L_t$ and H_t is aggregate human capital stock. Thus, the capitalists' life expectancy is higher than that of the peasants. Average human capital level of the workers of SF firms is such as $h_t \geq h^*$ i.e it is higher than that of the average in the world. There exist a threshold of human capital, h^* the one which the social planner is willing to make the peasant acquire. Peasants are endowed with low education levels i.e h_0 where $0 \leq h_0 < h^*$ which corresponds to a wage rate income below the threshold of standard of living i.e $w_0 < w^*$.

The Social planner taxes SF firms at the rate τ in order to finance learning by doing to eradicate poverty. Total time endowed by each peasant is normalized to unity, he spends *1-u* of his time to cultivate his living products and sells the rest for *$(1-u)\gamma h_0$* , where u, γ $\epsilon(0,1)$. Peasant spends the rest of his time i.e u to acquire additional human capital in a SF firm where he his remunerated at the income level equals to $u\tau h_0$ which came from fiscal policy on human capital accumulation. Therefore, total income of peasant is $\gamma(1-u)h_0+u\tau h_0=w_0<w^*$. This result means that, if the peasant human capital level is equal to zero, then the agent is a woman. We admit this assumption because some families in Africa may choose not to put their daughter in the education sector in order to take care of the household tasks. Then, if someone is endowed with zero human capital, the agent is a woman who lives with her husband income. There are the same number of women and men, so that a man can't have more than one wife.

The social planner exists during an infinite time, his budget constraint is expressed such as $L_t(uh_0)=\tau\Pi_t H_t$ which implies the following tax rate i.e

$$\tau = \frac{1}{\Pi_t}\left(\frac{L_t}{H_t}\right)uh_0 \qquad (1)$$

Where Π_t is the SF firms' aggregate income or aggregate profit, the peasant per-capita income is therefore:

$$\overline{w} = (uh_0)^2\frac{1}{\Pi_t}l_t - uh_0\gamma + \gamma h_0 \qquad (2)$$

Where $l_t = \dfrac{L_t}{H_t}$

Proposition 1 *let Πt be a per-capita SF firm's profit and τ a tax rate for human capital accumulation policy such as $\tau\in]0,1[$, then :*

If $\Pi_t = 4(l/\gamma)h_0$, the equilibrium wage rate income is unique i.e

$$w^* = 2\left(\frac{\gamma h_0}{\Pi_t}\right) \qquad (3)$$

Otherwise, if Π_t f $4(l/\gamma)h_0$ *then there exist multiple wage rate income equilibria* $\overline{w}^{max}$ *and* $\overline{w}^{min}$ *i.e*

$$\overline{w}^{max} = \frac{\gamma}{2} + \left(\frac{\gamma l h_0}{\Pi_t}\right)^{1/2} \text{ f } 0 \qquad (4)$$

$$\overline{w}^{min} = \frac{\gamma}{2} - \left(\frac{\gamma l h_0}{\Pi_t}\right)^{1/2} \text{ f } 0 \qquad (5)$$

Proof: we solve a second order equation where, if Π_t f $4(l/\gamma)h_0$, then there exist two positive roots which are $\overline{w}^{max}$ and $\overline{w}^{min}$ such that $\overline{w}^{max} > \overline{w}^{min}$, therefore, the wage rate income is minimum or maximal and corresponds to the professors' wage rate income or to the technicians wage rate income. If $\overline{w}^{min} \geq w*$ or $\overline{w}^{min} < w*$ then the lowest wage rate income is the one won by the peasant. Otherwise, if $\frac{\gamma}{2}$ p $\pm\left(\frac{\gamma l h_0}{\Pi_t}\right)^{1/2}$, then there doesn't exist a real wage rate income.

Otherwise, if $\dfrac{\gamma}{2} = \pm\left(\dfrac{\lambda h_0}{\Pi_t}\right)^{1/2}$, the wage rate income is a unique interior solution such that:

$$\hat{w} = w^* = 2\left(\dfrac{\lambda h_0}{\Pi_t}\right)^{1/2} \blacksquare$$

At the equilibrium of the labor force market of the MF firms, total labor supply equals L_t expressed such as total stock of peasants i.e $L_t = \sum_{i=1}^{N_L} L_{it}$ where per-capita peasant i human capital level is $h_{it} < h^*$ which is also per-capita human capital level. We also have the expression,

$N_t = N_L + N_H$ where $N_H = \sum_{i=1}^{i=N_H} H_{it} = H_t$.

The i SF firm uses aggregate human capital level stock $H_{it} \geq H^*$ as well as the exogenous technology A_{it} as a production input. There exist I SF *firms* where $I = \{1,2,..,m\}$ such that at each time period t the SF *firm* $\square$ $\{1,2,...,m\}$ uses its wealth X_{it} to finance the exogenous technology A_{it} and leaves the rest to finance peasant's learning by doing training while the production is holding as well as human capital inputs used. The production function of the *i* *SF firm* is a constant return function $F(H_{it}, A_{it})$.

Entrepreneurs of SF firms are also workers. International interest rate R is used both for lenders and the borrowers. Available income of SF firm *i* is

$$(1-\tau)X_{it} = Z_{it} - [G(A_{it}) + w_t H_{it}] \qquad (6)$$

Where Z_{it} is the sum of total capital borrowed added to personal SF firm's *i* income during time *t*, $G(A_{it})$ are the funds allocated to the exogenous technology spending. When Z_{it} is negative, then a part of the SF firm *i* wealth is invested into the international capital market. Because the SF firm *i* is limited in regard to the amount it can borrow in the market. Meaning that, Z_{it} must not exceed a fraction μ of total wealth acquired i.e $Z_{it} \leq \mu(1-\tau)X_{it}$ where $0<\mu<1$

SF firm i as a competitive equilibrium behavior, but is decision concerning demand factors are taken on the basis of their effects on the equilibrium wage rate i.e $w_{it} \geq w^*$.

At the modern labor force equilibrium, total labor force supply H_t equals total demand factors i.e $H_t = H_{it} + H_{-it}$

where

H_{-it} is the aggregate human capital demand of the other SF firms where $h_{it} \geq h^*$ is *per-capita* human capital level of per-agent working in SF firm i which has m skilled workers where $m \geq 1$. From equation (2), the wage rate income paid by the other firms equals w_t i.e

$$w_{it} = W_t(H_{it} + H_{-it}) = W_t(H_t) \geq w^* \qquad (7)$$

Therefore, the income of SF firm i in period t is such as (8) i.e

$$\Pi_{it} = (1 - \tau) F(Z_{it} + X_{it}, H_{it}) - W_t(H_t) H_{it} - G(A_{it}) - RZ_{it}$$
(8)

Where $w_t = W_t(H_t)$

Optimization of the profit of SF firm *i* determinate the inputs' costs i.e

$$w_t = W_t(H_t) = (1 - \tau)F'(Z_{it} + X_{it}, H_{it}) \qquad (9)$$

Where

$$0 < \tau < 1 - \left(\frac{W_t(H_t)}{F'(Z_{it} + X_{it}, H_{it})} \right)$$

Proposition 2: *the human capital level threshold which equivalent to the world average level is*

$$h^* = \left[\frac{F'(Z_{it} + X_{it}, H_{it})}{1 + F'(Z_{it} + X_{it}, H_{it}) \frac{ul_t}{\Pi_{it}} + (1 - u)\gamma} \right] \qquad (10)$$

Proof: replacing the wage rate income threshold by the expression of its value, we solve the equation which leads to

$$\overline{w} = w^* = 2 \left(\frac{\gamma h_0}{\Pi_t} \right)^{1/2} \quad \text{then} \quad \text{we} \quad \text{obtain} \quad \text{the}$$

expression of human capital level threshold, equation (10).

The increase of the profit increases human capital level threshold. Meaning, development necessitates more productive labor force because of new technology introduction. If we assume the Schumpeter creative/ destructive hypothesis where innovations are continuous, then labor demand is always more skilled. Otherwise, poverty settles and under development finds an explanation both at the local and the global society and economic plans.

4   THE DEMAND

Peasant spends his income on per-capita consumption along his living time i.e $w_0h_0=c_{it}$ whereas the SF firm skilled workers wage rate income is allocated between the first and the second period consumption i.e (c_{it}, d_{it+1}) and savings x_{it}

The intertemporal utility function of the agent is, (11) i.e

$$U = \ln(c_{it}) + \beta \ln(d_{it+1}) \qquad (11)$$

Where $d_{i,t+1}=0$ and $x_{it}=0$ for the peasant

In the first period, the agent budget constraint is such as $w_{it}=c_{it}+x_{it}$, in the second period, the agent consumes his whole savings i.e $d_{it+1}=(1+R)x_{it}$

The first order conditions of the optimization problem determinate the saving rate expressed by (12) i.e

$$x_{it} = \theta w_{it} \qquad (12)$$

Where $\theta=\beta/1+\beta$ is the marginal propensity to save of per-capita entrepreneur of the SF firm

5   THE GROWTH RATE

1) Equilibrium economic growth rate corresponds to the fraction of the saving rate such that $g_E=\theta$ and the natural growth rate or the growth rate of the population is $g_N=n$, *therefore we have several cases*

If $n<\theta$ then the economy leaves poverty, it is in transition between the take-off and development which means that development occurs

If $n\,\theta$ then the economy is kept in the poverty trap, it is located below the under development curve

If $n=\theta$ then the economy is leaving poverty, it is in transition to the take-off locus

Exogenous saving rate is the engine of long run development and growth

2) We introduce the exogenous technological change which moves according to the fraction σ where $0<\sigma<1$ like $(A_{t+1}-A_t)/A_t=\sigma$.

Therefore, the economic growth rate g is the sum of technological change growth rate and natural growth rates i.e $g=g_A+g_E=\theta+\sigma$

If $n<\theta+\sigma$, the economy leaves poverty, it is in transition between the take-off and the economic growth curve. Meaning development occurs with high velocity because demographic transition is done through education for all.

If $n\,\theta+\sigma$, the economy is kept in the poverty trap despite of the exogenous technological change because its power is not high enough since demographic transition didn't occur. The economy stagnates, remains poor and under developed.

If $n=\theta+\sigma$, the economy is no more in the poverty trap, it is at the take-off locus.

Last two previous cases are displayed by the development process curve. Growth is no more driven by the peasants because their high fecundity rate slows growth. Finally, the under development path leaves the poverty trap, through technology and human capital accumulation only if their rates are higher that natural rate.

Economic growth is endogenous if technolgy is determinate by the optimization of the economic agents when they try to increase they capital remuneration. This variable is associated with the firms' demand of capital, highlighted by the economic growth rate.

This model is a Solow (1956) growth model where the saving rate is exogenous. The model predicts convergence in the long run. We don't see that mechanics working because the economy is closed. Later on in the analysis, we'll open the country and thus results will differ.

We have illustrated analytically the Krugman (1994)'s idea of dualism of modern and traditional sectors based on Wigniolle (2005) where human capital is accumulated through learning by doing, thus poverty could be fought. Because the wage rate income increases with labor productivity increase. Indeed, learning by doing is able to increase the agents' well-being.

In parallel, firms' efficiency can be increased through technology improvements which may slow population increase and raise per-capita income. This analysis didn't include rural and urban migrations, but it dealt with migration since the peasant could work both in agriculture and in manufacture which are located in rural and urban areas respectively.

The purpose of the following chapter is to show in a descriptive way, that it is possible to introduce a well being collective criteria between the developed and the developing countries through cooperation between rich and poor countries. Cooperation we'll deal with in this study, consists on finding average levels of the crucial economic variables. Those crucial variables help to evaluate the economic agents well being, the economic development of the countries and demographic stability in age terms. We elaborate a synthesis of health problems faced by the both development and growth systems. The analysis evidences stable collective equilibria which establish an equivalency among economic agents in well being terms as well as among the countries in economic development levels terms as well as a demographic evolution. The book ends with an analytical analysis in order to elaborate future predictions.

Chapter N° 2

Development and Growth

1 INTRODUCTION

Europe and North America are facing great rise in obesity due to food disorders. There are 10 up to 27% of obese men and 38% of obese women in Europe. Recent studies predict that, in 2030, 100% of Americans will be obese. This affection generates many cancers, cardio vascular accidents and diabetes. As a public emergency problem, obesity necessitates great studies and indicators in order to lead to establish its complete eradication conditions. Obesity is also costly for public health-care and health insurances. The studies of the health cost predict that, in the future years, necessary funds will be too low to guarantee it access to the whole population [example of the French health-care system created in 1945]. The impossible stable life activity due to obesity raises pension funds matters because of the aging in developed countries. In parallel, the agents of Sub-Saharan Africa face low calorie food and high fecundity which reduces per-capita income.

Actual food crisis began in 2008 with high courses increase, increases poverty. According to the World Bank's february 15, 2011 announce, the impossibility of the poorest countries to feed their population results from the correlation between under development of productive capacities which creates global poverty on the one hand and of low human capital accumulation which causes local poverty on the other hand. Production in Sub-Saharan Africa reaches only 3.7% of the world GDP, his participation to the international exchange is only for 1.7% according to WTO[5] and according to Union Nations Commission for

---

[5] World Trade Organization

Africa, extreme poverty is at about 43% of the urban population against 53% of rural population, 59% of people live with less than 1 dollar per-day. The economic backwardness of poor countries is also caused by technological change absence. Life expectancy is reduced and the number of youth too high. In parallel, rich countries' population is facing aging, which is a good well being sign because life expectancy is increasing.

Therefore, through the concept of health, the study evidences foundations relate to well being collective criteria valid for all the countries. The purpose is to establish standard criteria which mixed development and growth in the agents' social conditions as well as in countries' wealth and demographic evolution. Since economic variables are stable, the economic systems move in a positive way to their long run locus. We present graphically the problem associated to the phenomenon we want to understand. Meaning, we elaborate stability principles of long run equivalency of the population as well as of the countries.

Associated to developed countries, growth concept is characterized by low fecundity rates and high human capital levels as well as high R&D investments. All those generate higher incomes than the average of the world. Indeed, the associated economic agents' incomes are located above the world average i.e the threshold standard of living. This situation is in developed countries' history related by early development economists as the resulting effects of demographic transition. But wealth has perverse effects like the rise both in obesity and in aging which raise some other questions such in the concern of the required funds to support social protection and pension funds. In parallel, unbounded increase of knowledge and technology leads to unbounded growth rate increase [Romer (1986), Lucas (1988)].

In contrast, Southern countries and specifically Sub-Saharan Africa, is always looking for development of the economy.

In contrast, Sub-Saharan economies are characterized by high fecundity rates [Dahan-Tsiddon (1998)] and low incentives to invest in human capital accumulation as well as in R&D. Those countries face local and global poverty as we've seen earlier [Deaton (2010), Azariadis-Drazen (1990), Romer (1990)]. To make the parallel with developed countries, the main effects of poverty are under eating and low life expectancy [World Bank, WHO[6]] increased by public health-care absence coupled to low incomes because labor productivity is too low as well as children quantity too high and low quality. Productive capacities under development are direct consequences of both low knowledge and technology in Sub-Saharan Africa. This situation can't allow

---

[6] World Health Organization

the poor economy converge to its long run development path [Lucas (1988)].

	Developed countries	Developing countries
Demography	High Aging	Under Aging
Fecundity rate	Low	High
Associated concept	Growth	Development
Impact on the agents	Obesity	Under nourishment
Labor	High	Low

productivity		
Human capital level	High	Low levels
Mortality rate	Low	High
Social protection	Costly	Absence
R&D investment	High investments	Low or zero

-figure 1 displays the history of growth and development. It highlights key events able to explain crucial points in growth and development evolutions.

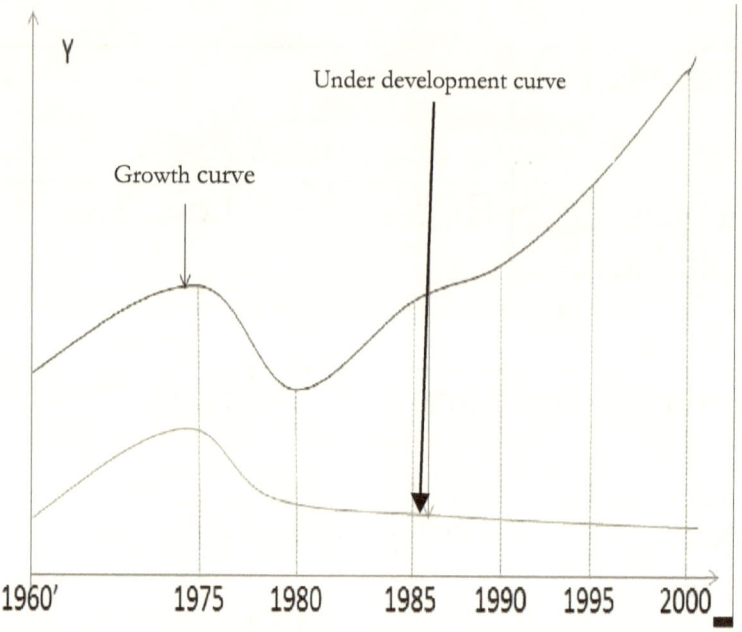

Y is measured in GDP

Over time, the economic gap between rich and poor countries keeps increasing in nations' wealth and in agents' income terms. Whereas the one keeps getting poor, the other keeps getting richer. In the 1970s, Africa's per-capita income was only for about nine times less than that of the OEDC countries. But this gap became twice bigger than before in the 1980s, this gap still increasing. But because wealth and poverty don't necessarily mean bad and good, the both situations can be improved through the collective well being criteria. The idea is: through health state, indicators can be created to estimate the best situation for all.

Synthetic image of both developed and development countries in terms of health can be highlighted such that:

-Obesity leads to health alteration and increases public health-care insurance because it reduces optimal work force.

-Population aging increases social security funds needed. Pension funds payment capacities are reduced too.

-Low fecundity rates and work capacity reduction, increase pension funds uncertainty.

-Low human capital levels are associated to low labor productivity. Quantity preferences to quality in the choice of the children decrease per-capita incomes. Indeed, demographic size evolution is higher than the equilibrium threshold.

-High human capital levels are associated to high labor productivity because quality is preferred to quantity in the choice of the children.

-Under nutrition increases health problems. Coupled to public funds absence for social security, life expectancy decreases are associated to poverty.

The well being collective criteria is obtained like equilibrium points of two symmetric systems highlighted by growth and development on the basis of health. Collective well being criteria can be summarized in three uniform concepts which are:

- *First,* there exist an equilibrium weight/ height ratio $r*$ which insures optimal health state $s*$ wherever be the agent lives. The ratio $r*$ is the average of the causing variables of obesity on the one part and of under nutrition on the other part. The aim of $r*$ is to provide an optimal body health state $s*$ allowing economies on social protection as well as on aging. Energy increase is necessary in working activity provided by $(r*,s*)$ which contributes to induce the economy converge to its long run growth added to the firms' productivity, public funds reach the equilibrium looked for. Therefore, the couple $(r*,s*)$ contribute to the process of the wealth of the nations. It decreases the uncertainty on the pension funds and on social security. This couple of variables contributes to a significant economic progress through the training of the economic agents in order to increase labor productivity.

We've seen in the previous chapter that reaching the thresholds of wage rate income and human capital level i.e $w*$, $h*$ eradicate under nutriment. Thus, allow peasant reach $(r*,s*)$ whatever be the economic system where he lives. This equilibrium couple eradicates obesity when the agent lives in a developed country. Indeed, because obesity is a decreasing curve in health state whereas health state is an increasing curve in good nourishment, the stable equilibrium exists.

-*Second,* the increase of the economic agents' human capital toward the threshold equivalent to the average world level, h^* protect the economic agents from poverty, specifically through the increase of the labor productivity at work. The idea is to make the agent subscribe a social insurance since he wins more income than the threshold of the living standard. Education supplies for all is important because more educated women in the economic system operate demographic transition, meaning that they prefer quality to quantity in the choice of the children

[Galor-Weil (2000)]. Demographic increase velocity is slowed [Dahan-Tsiddon (1998)] and per-capita income increased. Note that h^* exist and is stable because labor productivity function is monotone increasing in wage rate income in poor countries whereas, labor productivity is a decreasing function in wage rate income in rich countries because of the unbounded technological change. Since we accept the destructive/creative Schumpeter assumption in rich countries, it is true. Otherwise, if we refer to the certainty character of innovations of Segerström and Dinopoulos (1990) or of Romer (1990), then things are less obvious.

-*Third,* we develop foundations in order to establish population equilibrium in terms of the age $n*$. This equilibrium is the one on which the both economic systems will try to achieve in order to reduce the concentration of old people. The assumption of international labor mobility (migration of the young natives of developing countries to the OEDC countries) may contribute to finance pension funds in rich countries. Therefore, local poverty can also be fought through funds transfers from developed to developing countries [Rapoport et al (1997)] to the families in poor countries. The developing economies try to reach the average development level, d^*. Therefore, d is monotone increasing in n in rich countries, whereas, it is monotone decreasing in poor countries. Consequently, the stable equilibrium exists.

Définition1: collective well being criteria is « complete » if for a given economic agent endowed with a vector X such that X=(r,s,h) who lives in a country endowed with a couple of variables P such that P=(n,d) then, the assertions (1) and (2) are verified i.e.

(1)The economic agent satisfies the well being criteria i.e

$r \longrightarrow r*$

$s \longrightarrow s*$

$h \rightarrow h*$

(2)The country where lives the agent satisfies positive evolution of the economy i.e

$n \rightarrow n*$

$d \rightarrow d*$

Where r is the weight/ height ratio of the agent, s is health index associates to the weight/ height ratio. Average human capital level is h and demographic composition of the country is n, the economic development level is d and the sign * means optimal variable.

Définition2 : *the well being collective criteria is « partial » if for a given economic agent endowed with a vector X in a country with a couple of variables, P, X converge to X^** [labor mobility assumption is not accepted]

Collective well being criteria is a perfect foresight dynamics where growth and development converge to the same average locus. This criterias may be satisfied in this analysis through coordinate efforts of the rich and the poor countries. More precisely, we establish equity economic principles for a positive evolution of the human beings. Figure 2 displays the situation described above.

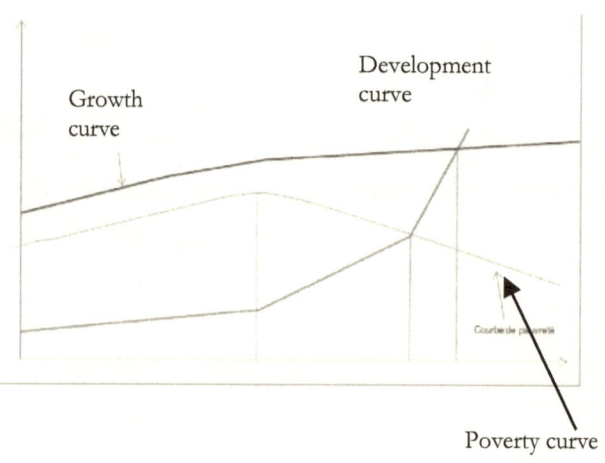

Poverty curve

2 THE ANALYTIC METHODOLOGY

In order to establish principles to ensure convergence of *(d,n)* to *(d*,n*)*, we fix the ideas like following :

If *n<n** then demographic structure is such that old people are too much

If *n≻n** then demographic structure is such that young people are too much

If *n=n** then demographic structure is at its best level

We do the same thing for economic development i.e

If *d<d** then the economic development level is too low

If *d≻d** then the economic development level is higher than the threshold

If *d=d** then the economic development level is at its best level

The following array links *d* to *n*

	$d<d*$	$d>d*$	$d=d*$
$n>n*$	$n>n*;d<d*=$	$n>n*;d>d*$	$n>n*;d=d*$
$n<n*$	$n<n*; d<d*$	$n<n*;d>d*$	$n<n*;d=d*$
$n=n*$	$n=n*; d<d*$	$n=n*;d>d*$	$n=n*;d=d*$

Events accounting:

According to the previous array, the sets which deserve corrections are denoted: A, B, C where

A deserves both corrections in regard to n (which must decrease) and to d (which must increase) in their average levels because they are under leveled.

B deserves a correction in regard to n in its average level because d is well located

C deserves a correction in regard to d in its average level because n is well located

$$\text{Where}$$

$$A=\{(n>n*;d<d*)\}$$
$$B=\{(n<n*;d>d*),(n>n*;d>d*),(n>n*;d=d*)\}=B_1\cup B_2\cup B_3$$
$$C=\{(n<n*;d<d*),(n=n*;d<d*)\}=C_1\cup C_2$$

The sets which ensure the take-off and growth are respectively denoted: O, E i.e

$O=\{(n=n*;d=d*)\}$ is the take-off locus

$E=\{(n=n*;d>d*),(n<n*;d=d*)\}$ is an increasing function $d=f(n)$ for $n\leq n*$

Therefore:

-An economy located between O and E is in transition from development to growth

-An economy located between under development curve and O is leaving under development for development

-An economy located between under development curve and the point O, is in transition to the take-off locus

-An economy located below under development curve is kept in a poverty trap

-An economy located above growth curve achieves its long run growth in technological change, this country is rich

Figure 3 highlights economic situations which deserve corrections in order to construct economic indicators i.e A,B,C

-The take-off locus is represented by O

-The point E corresponds to the dynamics of the developed country (see figure 4)

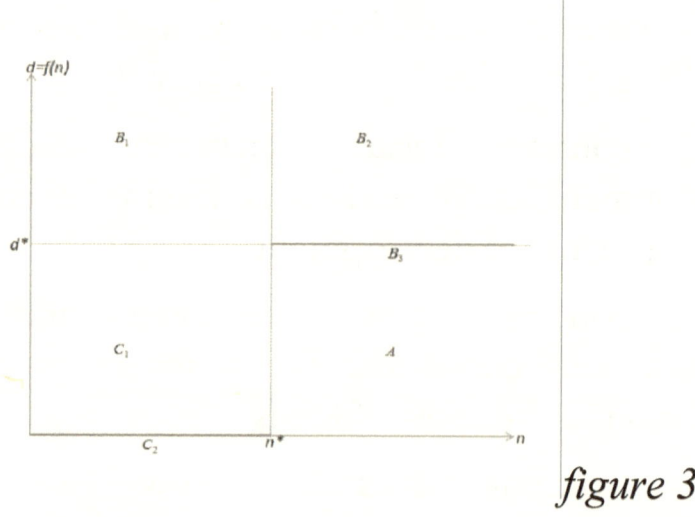

figure 3

To obtain the convergence of *(r,s)* to *(r*,s*)*, we proceed like following:

If (r>r)∩(s<s*)*, the agent is obese

If (r<r)∩(s<s*)*, the agent is under nourished

If (r≤r*)∩(s≥s*), the agent is in good health

If (r≥r*)∩(s≻s*), the agent is overweighted

Equivalently

If h=0, the agent is not scholarly educated

If h≻h *, the agent is engineer or professor

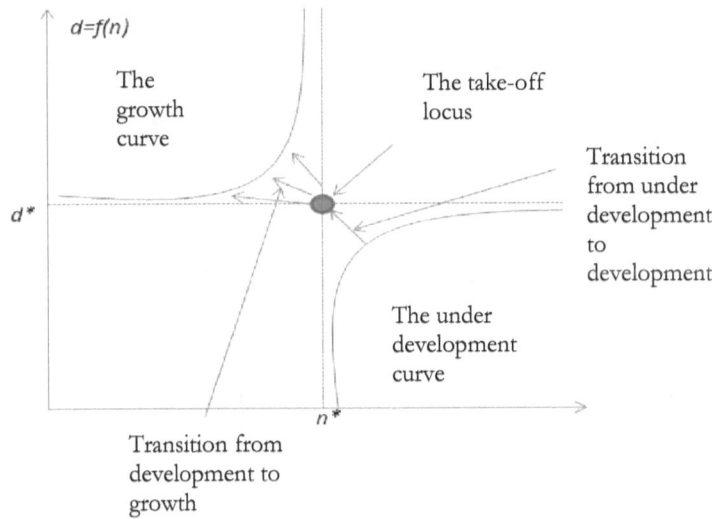

d=f(n)

The growth curve

The take-off locus

Transition from under development to development

d^*

The under development curve

n^*

Transition from development to growth

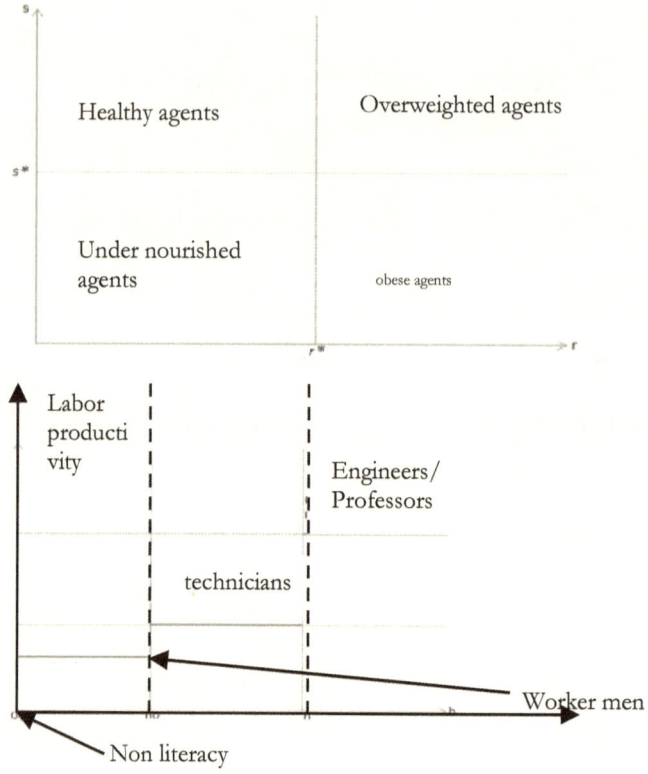

If $0 < h_0 < h*$, the agent is a peasant or a worker man

If $h_0 < h \leq h*$, the agent is a technician

After the descriptive study of the well being collective criteria just viewed above, we study now the same concept analytically in the next chapter.

PART II

The foundations of growth for economic development

The theoretical foundations of the relationships between growth and development

1 INTRODUCTION

This chapter models analytically the situation viewed in the previous chapter. We present the economic environment of the study quite fast because the last chapter provided already useful definitions.

2 THEORETICAL ANALYSIS

There exist two countries, where the one is developed and the other is not developed yet. In the both countries, we can find well being agents as well as overweight agents. But obese agents are only in the developed country whereas under nourished agents are only in the developing country.

The economic policy we are dealing with is mainly focused both on under nourished and obese agents. Obesity and under nourishment necessitate more attention because they have an impact on growth and development. Similarly, technicians, worker men and/ or peasants are in the both economic systems of the poor and of the rich countries. But professors and engineers are only in the developed country whereas non alphabet agents who mostly are women are only in the developing country. Finally, there are many old people in the rich country and many young people in the poor country.

The analysis is a macroeconomic model based on growth theory where exist a developed country D and a developing country D^{inf}. The economies are opened and each of them as a social planner, firms and economic agents.

Each economic agent makes one or several well specified tasks we're going to precise as the model is being built.

-The social planner

●the social planner of D is focused on obesity and aging. His task is to establish an optimal health state level, $(r*,s*)$ which decrease uncertainty on the finance of the pension funds as well as of social security. Physical activities are proposed by social security department and supported by taxes on bad quality food producing firms because it increases obesity risks. In other words, there exist an endogenous production threshold y^* which divides consumptions' good quality between low quality consumption goods, $c<c*$ which increases obesity risks because its production function is located below the production threshold i.e $y<y*$, whereas good quality consumption good are such that, $c\geq c*$ and prevent the agent from obesity because its production function quality is located above the threshold $y\geq y*$. Moreover, if the country D introduces labor mobility assumption after

the reach of $(r*,s*)$, then pension funds financial support is guarantee. The last case deals with the brain drain literature not studied in this book.

●The social planner of D^{inf} is mostly focused on under nourishment and non skilled labor training. He wants to reach the optimal health state level $(r*,s*)$ in order to increase life expectancy of the economic agents. Through the agents' training, labor productivity may be increased to achieve the average human capital level, $h*$ which protects the agent from poverty. Moreover, the social planner's goal is also to reach the average economic development level $d*$.

More precisely, human capital accumulation is supported by fiscal policy from low quality consumption goods' taxes. Those funds are given to good consumptions' firms which production quality is located above the threshold i.e $y \geq y*$ in order to train the unskilled agents during the production process. The purpose is to increase human capital level h_0 at the average level i.e $h_0 \rightarrow h*$. Doing this, the social planner expects the poor agents to get a social insurance through the increase of their wage rate income due to their human capital level increase.

If the firms of the developing countries import developed country's technology because R&D is absent, then $d < d*$ at the beginning and the economy begins to increase and converge to the take-off locus O. But the economic dynamics moves from development to growth only if $d \rightarrow d*$.

The government pressure on non efficient firms as well as competition among firms lead to continuous technology innovation in order to increase consumption goods' quality. Therefore, economic development dynamics is a process wider than economic structures change because of the implication of sustainability.

-The production sector

●the country D is composed of three exogenous sectors i.e not modeled.

The research sector uses human capital and new knowledge to develop new innovations.

The intermediate good production sector applies results obtained by the research sector to generate new production methods i.e equipments goods to use in the final good production sector.

The final good production sector uses human capital inputs, labor force as well as equipments to produce goods which will be consumed or saved.

●The production sector of D^{inf} possess intermediate and final good production sectors only.

The intermediate production sector uses discarded developed country's technology obtained at low cost for the needs of the final good production sector.

The final good production sector uses average human capital as well as discarded equipments to produce consumption goods which can be consumed or saved.

Firms' convergence on production quality levels through innovation and technological change set the economic dynamics to the take-off locus at the first step. Then the economic dynamics goes to the growth curve after $d \rightarrow d*$.

Food taxes support training while production is holding in order to get a social insurance as well as to reach the equilibrium health state $(r*, s*)$ since $h \rightarrow h*$ and then $w = w*$, agent's wage rate income converges to the threshold of the living standard.

-Economic agents of D and D^{inf} need to go from (r,s) to $(r*,s*)$ mostly because of obesity and under nourishment respectively.

Agents of D^{inf} are trained in order to achieve an average human capital level corresponding to $h*$. Therefore, the women of this country are drained to the labor market too like the men because they are now endowed with a basic conventional human capital level. Indeed, demographic transition occurs necessarily because of the opportunity cost of the children. Thus quality is preferred to quantity in the choice of the children. Fecundity rate decreases and per-capita income increases and well being through social insurance acquired with an income higher or equal to the threshold of the living standard. Consequently, life expectancy is higher.

The scientific contribution holds on the following points :

-The analysis summarizes the specific problems of both the developed and the developing countries through the same criteria. Meaning, we deal with well being issues in order to provide collective indicators of "substainability" and the economy.

-We establish universal laws which found development economics as well as long run growth

-This study is a contribution to the endogenous growth theory which deals with health as well as to economic development. Its originality holds on a parallel model which links established a unified growth and development theories.

-The study is also a contribution to the theory of development economics which highlight criteria establishing a unity with other economic systems through the equilibrium necessity.

-The study rise the theory of development economics which fall in the mid 1970s [Krugman (1994)]

-It is a synthesis of the economic dilemmas faced by the development purpose in order to establish stability where health is the variable which makes the link among economic systems differentials.

-Both development and growth theories get inside a new paradigm which links them to health after sustainability in this 21th century because growth and ecology in macroeconomic models is only a hidden vector like a black box.

In conclusion, the study is an endogenous growth model which incorporates health and human capital [Romer (1986), Lucas (1988), King-Rebelo (1987)], as well as technological change [Eicher (1996), Romer (1990), Stockey (1988)]. We also deal with fiscal policy [King-Rebelo (1987), Rebelo (1987), Ortiguerira (1993)]. The study is also added of the relationship between growth environment components [Bovenberg-Smulders (1995), Stockey (1998), Brock-Taylor (2010)] to constitute a unified macroeconomic model.

Growth literature has almost touched all the fields except health which still in its infancy [Goel (2006)]. Most of the existing literature is empirical inquiring with the factors which cause obesity over time [Cutler et al (2003), Chou et al (2004), Lakdawalla et al (2005), Rashad et al (2006)]. Few articles focus on individual decisions to consume high caloric food to study their impact on health and life expectancy. Philipson-Posner (1999) is a rational choice model of food consumption to study the impact of weight on technological change which reduces both the food price and physical exercises quantities. Levy (2002) is a dynamic model of the choice of a risky life caused by food consumption excess in order to determinate the optimal weight not to achieve. Gideon et al (2009) uses fiscal policy and subsidies as well as rational choice of the calorie to take in order to determinate the equilibrium weight when the agent practices physical exercises. Fiscal policy may increase obesity through the reduction of time spent in physical activities. Zon-Muysken (2001) is the first article which integrates growth in order to increase health. This work mainly focuses on aging as well as its impact on growth and labor productivity. In that model, health is viewed such as a variable directly linked to human capital accumulation.

This analysis focuses on that advanced knowledge to introduce itself like a synthesis of growth and development economics through health. It constitutes a unified analysis of health in an endogenous growth model in order to provide theoretical foundations of the stability of the key economic variables. The main purpose is to provide a collective unified well being criteria where development and growth are no more knowledge result only but well being necessity as well.

The extension of the study to institution imperfections in Sub-Saharan Africa introduces bias and uncertainty on the economic policy success. In parallel, developed countries face obesity due to consumption habits or life styles of the agents which are more food and less physical exercises as well as technological change in leisure i.e computer games, internet, and the access of a car despite of a bike or a bus which decrease obesity.

The Production

In open economies, the respective firms of the developing and the developed countries are:

$$N_t^{\bar{d},L} + N_t^{\bar{d},H} = 1 \qquad (1)$$

$$N_t^{d,L} + N_t^{d,H} = 1 \qquad (2)$$

The previous equations mean that efficient and non efficient firms represent total firms of the countries. The index $\bar{d}$ represents the poor country variables and the index d represents the developed country's variables. In the countries, the budget constraint of the social planner is such that:

$$\tau_t^j y_t^{i,L} N_t^i = u h_0^i L_t^i \qquad (3)$$

The previous social planner's budget constraint determinate the tax rate such that

$$\tau_t^j = u \left(\frac{L_t^i}{N_t^i} \right) \frac{h_0^i}{y_t^{i,L}} \qquad (4)$$

$\left(\tau_t^j \right)_{\lambda=d,\bar{d}}$ is the tax rate the social planner imposes to the non efficient firms i.e firms which production quality is located such that $y_t^{i,L} < y^*$ because they sell food which creates obesity or under nourishment. Therefore, non efficient and efficient firms' available incomes are respectively expressed such that:

$$\left(1-\tau_t^i\right)y_t^{i,L} \qquad (5)$$

$$\tau_t^i y_t^{i,L} + y_t^{i,H} \qquad (6)$$

The social planner transfers those funds to the efficient firms which satisfy $y_t^{i,H} \geq y*$ because the quality of their products is higher or equal to the threshold required to establish the equilibrium weight/ height ratio $r*$ leading to the equilibrium health state $s*$. Per-capita capital of the firms are respectively for the non efficient and the efficient firms such that:

$$k_{t+1}^{i,L} = s^{i,L}\left(1-\tau_t^i\right)y_t^{i,L} \qquad (7)$$

$$k_{t+1}^{i,H} = s^{i,H}\left(y_t^{i,H} - \tau_t^i y_t^{i,L}\right) \qquad (8)$$

$s^{i,L}$ and $s^{i,H}$ are the respective non efficient and efficient firms' marginal propensity to save. Interest rate is exogenous and capital can be borrowed or invested to the international capital market at a rate, R which corresponds to the lending and the borrowing rates respectively.

Non efficient and efficient sectors of production employ human capital, $H_t^{\bar{d}}$ and both of the firms are in competitive markets. Average per-capita capital stock is then

$$k_t = \bar{s}\left[\left(\frac{1}{1-uh_0^i l_t^i}\right)y_t - 1\right]\text{f } 0 \qquad (9)$$

Functional forms of the respective per-capita production functions are expressed by (10) and (11) i.e

$$y_t^{i,L} = l_t^{i,\alpha} \qquad (10)$$

$$y_t^{i,H} = k_t^{i,\beta} \qquad (11)$$

Where $0<a, \beta<1$ and $a+\beta=1$, T_t^i is land

$$l_t^i = \frac{L_t^i}{T_t^i}$$

$$h_t^i = \frac{H_t^i}{K_t^{i,H}}$$

Thus, optimization of the respective profits expresses per-capita wage rate incomes, equations (12) and (13) i.e

$$w_t^{i,L} = \alpha l_t^{i,\alpha-1} \qquad (12)$$

$$w_t^{i,H} = \beta k_t^{i,\beta-1} \qquad (13)$$

The resulting wage rate income is then

$$w_t^i = \left(\frac{\beta}{\alpha}\right) \frac{y_t^{i,\beta-1}}{y_t^{i,\alpha-1}} \qquad (14)$$

Relationship between per-capita capital and the wage rate incomes is expressed by (15) i.e

$$k_t^i = \bar{s}\left[\left(\frac{\alpha}{\beta\left[1-uh_0^i l_t^i\right]}\right)w_t^i - 1\right] f\ 0 \qquad (15)$$

Where

$$k_t^i = \frac{k_t^{i,\beta-1}}{l_t^{i,\alpha-1}}$$

$$\alpha f\ \beta\left[1-uh_0^i l_t^i\right] \approx \beta$$

The increase of relative wages increase relative per-capita capital and create inequalities access to the capital market as well as to the education sector where human capital is accumulated. Therefore, human capital level increase conditioned health through social security needs and decreases inequalities. Finally, per-capita capital is expressed by (16) i.e

$$k_t^i = \bar{s}\left[\frac{\alpha}{\beta}w_t^i - 1\right] \qquad (16)$$

Proof: per-capita capital and the wage rate income in the long run are:

$$k_t^i = k \quad \forall i \in N$$

$$w_t^i = w^i \quad \forall i \in N$$

We obtain

$$k^i = \bar{s}\left[\frac{\alpha}{\beta}w^i - 1\right]$$

3   THE DEMAND

Economic agents have a utility function which depends on per-capita consumption and per-capita health state expressed by the equation (17) i.e

$$U = \ln\left(c_t^i\right) + \gamma^j \ln\left(s_t^i\right) \qquad (17)$$

Obese and the under nourished agents live one period of time only and during this period of time, they spend their income in good consumption and in medical-care for their health state. Obese agents have a social security but their health state is too low to allow them live more than one period.

Other agents live two periods of time because they are not peasant and/or obese and under nourished. Thus they have a private social security in the developing country whereas in the developed country, the obese agents' social security is public.

The first order conditions of the optimization problem determinate the equilibrium levels of per-capita consumption and of per-capita health state which also is medical-care cost, then they determinate the weight/ height ratio $r*$. Health state is a function of the weight/ length ratio i.e $s*=r*-\delta c*$ which determinate the optimal solutions or per-capita consumption and per-capita health state i.e

$$c^{*,i} = \frac{1}{1+\gamma} w^{i,H} \qquad (18)$$

$$s^{*,i} = \frac{\gamma}{1+\gamma} w^{i,H} \qquad (19)$$

We determinate now, the weight/ height ratio i.e

$$r^{*,i} = \frac{\gamma+\delta}{1+\gamma} w^{i,H} \qquad (20)$$

International labor market equilibrium assumes the equality of the aggregate human capital to the threshold of the average world human capital i.e $H^i = H^*$. We obtain also the same thing in the concern of the wage rate income among the skilled and the non skilled labor i.e

$$w^{d,H} = w^{\bar{d},H} = w^{H,*} \qquad (21)$$

$$w^{d,L} = w^{\bar{d},L} = w^{L,*} \qquad (22)$$

Long run labor market equilibrium determinate the collective well being indicators expressed by equations (23), (24) and (25) i.e

$$r^* = \frac{\gamma + \delta}{1 + \gamma} w^{H,*} \qquad (23)$$

$$s^* = \frac{\gamma}{1 + \gamma} w^{H,*} \qquad (24)$$

$$k^* = \bar{s} \left[\frac{\alpha}{\beta} w^{H,*} - 1 \right] \qquad (25)$$

Indeed $(r*,s*)$ determinate is the average of what causes the obesity to what causes the under nourishment because those foods are provided by the low quality good consumptions production.

Capital market equilibrium leads to $w_{t+1}=w_t=w*$ $\forall t \in N$ because the skilled agents' total time is normalized to unity, they spend a fraction of their time u to the efficient firms for training in developing countries and the same time to developed country to practice physical exercises. Worker spends their remaining time $1-u$ in good production of the non efficient production sector which is exogenous in the model i.e not modeled.

3 THE GROWTH RATE

Non efficient firms' per-capita growth rate is the difference between capital growth and natural growth rate i.e

$$g_k^L \approx g_y^L - g_l^L \qquad (26)$$

If g_y^L f g_l^L which means, the capital growth rate is higher than natural growth rate, the economy is taking-off

If $g_y^L < g_l^L$ which means, the capital growth rate is lower than natural growth rate, the economy is kept in a Malthusian poverty trap with under development of productive capacities

If $g_y^L = g_l^L$ which means, the capital growth rate is equal to the natural growth rate, the economy is in transition between under development and take-off

Efficient firms' growth rate is the sum of the capital growth rate and the natural growth rate i.e

$$g_k^H \approx g_y^H + g_l^L \qquad (27)$$

If $g_k^H \text{ f } g_y^H + g_l^L$ which means, the effective efficient firm growth rate is higher than the sum of capital and natural growth rates, therefore the economy is in transition from development to growth

If $g_k^H \text{ p } g_y^H + g_l^L$ which means, the effective efficient firm growth rate is lower than the sum of capital and natural growth rates, therefore the economy still located between under development and the take-off

If $g_k^H = g_y^H + g_l^L$ which means, the effective efficient firm growth rate is equal to the sum of capital and natural growth rates, therefore the economy is being stable i.e

$$g_k^H = g_y^H + g_l^L + g_k^L$$

Global growth rate is expressed by equation (28)

$$g = g_y^H + g_y^L \qquad (28)$$

Global growth rate is the sum of the efficient and the non efficient firms' growth rates it may be under developed, developed or high it depends on the locus where firms are located in the plane.

4   DETERMINATION of the equilibria respectively in age and in development economics terms i.e $(n*, d*)$

We assume that, the developing country has a fraction of young people q and a fraction of old people $1-q$. In parallel, the developed country has a fraction of young $1-p$ and a fraction of old people p where $q>1-p$ such that $q>1-p$ where $0<p,q<1$. Indeed we have the two following implications

$$qN_t^{\bar{d}} \geq (1-p)N_t^d$$

$$(1-q)N_{t-1}^{\bar{d}} \leq pN_{t-1}^d$$

The above implications mean that the young people of the poor country are higher than the old people of the developed country or they are equivalent. We note the same thing between the old people of the poor country and the young people of the developed country, they are equivalent.

Assuming that rich and poor countries demographic variable move at the same constant rate $n*$ then according to the previous inequalities, we determinate its optimal level expressed by equation (29) i.e

$$n* = \frac{N_t^{\bar{d}} - N_t^d}{(1-p)N_{t-1}^d - qN_{t-1}^{\bar{d}}} \qquad (29)$$

To determinate optimal development level, $d*$ we assume that the developing country's development level is lower than that of the threshold i.e $d_1 < d*$ but the developed country's development level is higher than that of the threshold i.e $d_2 \succ d*$. Consequently, the average development level of both the developed and the developing countries $d*$ is an arithmetic variable expressed such that

$$d* = (d_1 + d_2)/2$$

Because the capital marginal returns in the developing country are lower than that of the developed country, then there is convergence because it is an exogenous technological change model where absolute convergence occurs in the long run. Indeed our model is a Solow (1956) model because technology is not chosen by agents who maximize their profits. Otherwise, the developing country's economy will be unable to converge to the same growth rate as the developed country because convergence will be conditional to some variables.

Conclusion

This analysis began with the review of the literature of the firms in developing countries in order to evaluate the causality of poverty and under development of productive capacities. The aim of the study is the rise of standard development economics through a formal model. The purpose is to introduce development economics in growth literature as well as levy confusion between poverty trap and the productive capacity's under development. We finally conclude that local poverty is caused by low incentives to invest in human capital accumulation and global poverty is caused by non efficient firms. We then model the idea of Krugman (1994) of the dualism in production due to Lewis (1954) in order to increase human capital level of the peasant because their wage rate income will increase to allow them to win a wage rate income at least equal to the threshold and demographic transition will occurrence. Then, to relate the developing country to the developed country, we established an examination of the key economic variables shared by the one and the other systems to see how the equilibrium can be found. Based on health, a link is established between developed and developing countries. Then, we try to understand how health works in the both systems through the growth theory. It was done both statistically and analytically. Finally we determinate the well being collective criteria based on health variables valid for all the systems in the world.

This analysis can be extended to the inclusion of the government intervention more explicitly than in this study in order to make the poor economy gets out of the poverty trap where it is kept. This model focuses mostly on the firms and the household and economic development was not explicitly modeled.

Bibliographie

Aghion, P. and Howitt, P., Théorie de la Croissance, 1998, Dunod

Assidon, Elsa, 2002, Les Théories Economiques du développement, Repères, la Découverte

Brunel, S., Le Sud dans la Nouvelle Economie Mondiale, PUF

Burki, A. and Terrel, D., 1998, Measuring production efficiency of small firms in Pakistan, World Development, 26 (1), 155-169

Cass, D., Optimum Growth in an Aggregate Model of Capital Accumulation, Review of Economic Studies, 32, 233-240

Chou, S.Y., Grossman., M., Saffer, H., 2003, An economic analysis of adult obesity results from the behavioral risk factor surveillance system, Journal of health economics, 23 (3), 565-587

Collins, J. and Porras, J., 1994, Built to last: Successful habits of visionary companies, New-York: Harper and Collins

Cutler, D.M., Glaeser, E.L., Shapiro, J.M., 2003, Why have Americans become more obese? Journal of Economic Perspectives, 17 (3), 93-118

Doquier, F. and Rapoport, H., 2010, Glabalization, Brain-Drain and Development, Journal of Economic Literature

Docquier, F; and Marfouk, A., 2006, International Migration by educational attainement, Palgrave Mc Millan New-york

Downing, J. and Daniels, L., 1992, The growth and dynamics of women enterpreneurs in Southern Africa, GEMINI, technical report number 27, Washigton D.C. US AID

Fleming, J.M., 1955, External Economics and the doctrine of Balanced Growth, Economic Journal, June

Goel, R.K., 2006, Obesity: an economic and financial perspective, Journal of Economics and Finance, 30 (3), 317-324

Goldmark, L. and Barber, T., 2005, Trade micro and small enterprises and global value chain. AMAP report number 25, Washington D.C. US AID

Hirschman, A., 1958, The Stategy of Economic Development, New Haven, Conn: Yale University Press

Hugon, P., 1999, L'Economie de l'Afrique, Repères, la Découverte

King, R. G., Rebelo, S., 1990, Public Policy and Economic Growth: Developing Neoclassical Implications, NBER Working Paper n°3338

Krugman, 1994, The Fall and rise of Development economics, working paper, p.1-13

Koopmans, T. , 1965, On the Concept of Optimal groxth, The Econometris Approach to Development Planning, Chicago

Levy, A., 2002, Rational eating: can it lead to overweightness or underweightness? , Journal of health economics, 21 (5), 887-899

Lewis, W.A., 1954, Economic Development with unlimited supplies of Labor, The Manchester School, May

Loeadholm, C., 2002, Small firm dynamics: Evidence from Africa and Latin America, Small Business Economics, 18 (3), 227-242

Lucas R.E., On the Mechanics of Economic Development, Journal of Monetary Economics, 22, 3-42

Myrdal, G; 1957, Economic Theory and Under-developed Regions, London, Duckworth

Parker, J., 1995, Partnes of Business Growth, Micro and Small Enteprises in Kenya, ph.D Dissertation

Philipson, T.J., Posner, R.A., 1999, The long-run growth in obesity as a function of technological change. Working Paper 7423. National Bureau of Economic Research, Cambrige, MA

Rashad, I., Grossman, Chou, S.Y., 2006, The Super Size of America: an economic estimation of body mass index and obesity in adults, Eastern Economioc Journal, 32 (1), 133-148

Romer, P., 1986, Increasing Returns and Long Run Growth, Journal of Political Economy 94, 1002-1037

Roseinstein-Rodant, P., 1943, Problem of Industrialization od Eastern and Sout-Easter Europe, Economic Journal, June

Tan, H. and Batra, G., 1995, technical efficiency of SME, World Bank, Washington D.C

Wigniolle, B., 2005, Does Imperfect Competition Foster Capital Accumulation in a Developing Economy?, Cahier de la MSE

Young, A., 1928, Increasing Returns and Economic Progress, December

Zon, A., Muysken, J., 2001, Health and endogenous Growth, Journal of Health Economics, 20, 169-1